SMOKY MOUNTAIN HYMNS

*Beautiful Scenes and Timeless Hymns
from the Great Smoky Mountains*

SMOKY MOUNTAIN HYMNS

*Beautiful Scenes and Timeless Hymns
from the Great Smoky Mountains*

Written and Edited by Frederick Julian Richardson

Brentwood, Tennessee

Published MCMXCIII in Brentwood, Tennessee, by Brentwood Books

ISBN 1-55897-569-1

Written and edited by Frederick Julian Richardson

Design by Tal Howell Design

Project Coordinator, Jackie L. Hall

Photo credits: ©A.J. Spillman pp. 6-15, 18,19,22-25,30-31
              ©Dill Beaty pp.16-17, 20-21, 26-27, 28, 29

Scripture taken from the HOLY BIBLE, KING JAMES VERSION

Printed in Mexico

FOREWORD

The hymns of the Smoky Mountains are a rich heritage handed down to us by those hard-working, God-fearing early settlers who carved out their livelihood in one of the most beautiful places on God's green earth. They came from Scotland and Ireland, Switzerland, Germany and many other countries to a land which promised freedom to worship their God and the opportunity to see hard work rewarded in this life.

These are songs of hope, songs of faith, songs of God's love and His heavenly promises. We invite you to enjoy with us now the awe-inspiring beauty of the Smokies and the Spirit-inspired words of our forefathers' favorite hymns.

WHAT A FRIEND WE HAVE IN JESUS

What a Friend we have in Jesus,
All our sins and griefs to bear!
What a privilege to carry
Everything to God in prayer!
O what peace we often forfeit,
O what needless pain we bear,
All because we do not carry
Everything to God in prayer!

"My voice shalt thou hear in the morning, O Lord; in the morning
will I direct my prayer unto thee, and will look up" (Psalm 5:3).

It is an early fall morning in the Smokies. There are only the sounds of birds in the trees and water gently rippling over the smooth, worn stones. What do we see? It is up to us. We choose our perspective.

We can choose to look on such a scene and see only the negative. We might say, "Oh, the leaves are turning; winter and its cold barrenness will too soon overtake the landscape." "The water is low over the rocks; we are in need of rain." Or we might say: "There is no bright sun shining; I guess it's going to rain again today."

But there is another perspective. We might look and say, "How beautiful are the leaves' colors!" "Oh, how wonderful that the river isn't flooding; I can wade across and see what is on the other side!" "How cool and refreshing it is in the morning before the sun comes out and heats up the day!"

Those are the choices we make each day. Let's take the second perspective on our lives and enter each day with our Friend Jesus, taking everything to Him in prayer so that He can give us Heaven's glasses to view the world around us.

AMAZING GRACE

Amazing grace! How sweet the sound,
That saved a wretch like me!
I once was lost, but now am found,
Was blind, but now I see.

'Twas grace that taught my heart to fear,
And grace my fears relieved;
How precious did that grace appear
The hour I first believed.

Thro' many dangers, toils, and snares,
I have already come;
'Tis grace hath bro't me safe thus far,
And grace will lead me home.

When we've been there ten thousand years,
Bright shining as the sun,
We've no less days to sing God's praise
Than when we first begun.

"How precious did that grace appear the hour I first believed." Do you remember that moment, that hour when you first believed? Did you laugh, did you shout, did you cry tears of joy, tears streaming forth from your very heart of hearts? Were you alone in your prayer closet, were you in church, were you on a mountaintop or deep in a valley? Did you fall to your knees before the God of your salvation?

However God chose to work your salvation, take a few moments now to reflect back on it. Bask in the sweetness of the sound of His Amazing Grace. Feel again the joy, the relief, the exhilarating release from sin as you sing again, "I once was lost, but now am found, was blind, but now I see."

Dear Lord, thank you for my salvation. Please remind me daily that
it is only by Your Amazing Grace that I will ever see that heavenly place,
that I will ever see Your face "Bright shining as the sun."

CHURCH IN THE WILDWOOD

*There's a church in the
valley by the wildwood,
No lovelier place
in the dale.
No spot is so dear
to my childhood,
As the little brown
church in the vale.*

*Oh, come to the church
in the wildwood,
Oh, come to the
church in the vale.
No spot is so dear
to my childhood,
As the little brown
church in the vale.*

What greater gift can we give our children than precious memories of moments spent in God's house of worship? It doesn't have to be a quaint little building in a picture-postcard setting; it can be an inner-city mission, a large suburban church or rented space in a high school auditorium. It is not the "where" that matters, but what takes place inside.

Our children will remember the love shared, the songs sung, and the evidence of the Holy Spirit's presence as He changes lives before their eyes. If we provide them with such a place, then we will see God's promise fulfilled:

"Train up a child in the way he should go: and when he is old, he will not depart from it" (Proverbs 22:6).

WHEN WE ALL GET TO HEAVEN

Sing the wondrous love of Jesus,
Sing His mercy and His grace;
In the mansions bright and blessed
He'll prepare for us a place.

While we walk the pilgrim pathway
Clouds will overspread the sky;
But when trav'ling days are over,
Not a shadow, not a sigh.

Let us then be true and faithful,
Trusting, serving every day;
Just one glimpse of Him in glory
Will the toils of life repay.

Onward to the prize before us!
Soon His beauty we'll behold;
Soon the pearly gates will open,
We shall tread the streets of gold.

When we all get to heaven,
What a day of rejoicing that will be!
When we all see Jesus,
We'll sing and shout the victory.

The message of this hymn is not just wishful thinking. It is a message of faith, of hope, of endurance, of trust in a loving heavenly Father.

This message is the greatest truth the world has ever known! When the hymnwriter wrote, "He'll prepare for us a place," she was simply repeating her heavenly Father's loving promise. So let us all embrace this thought. Let's open our eyes. Let's shout from our rooftops for all of the world to hear:

"Look up, and lift up your heads, for your redemption draweth nigh!"

GLORY TO HIS NAME

O precious fountain that saves from sin,
I am so glad I have entered in;
There Jesus saves me and keeps me clean;
Glory to His Name!

Glory to His name!
Glory to His name!
There to my heart was the blood applied;
Glory to His name!

"The life of the flesh is in the blood"
(Leviticus 17:11).

The Smokies are glorious in the fall when the leaves burst into a riot of colors. From summer's all encompassing green they transform into brilliant reds, subtle oranges and sunshine yellows. What causes this artistic transformation reminds us of Jesus' sacrifice for us on the cross.

For us to enjoy the beauty of fall leaves, they must die. Just as we have blood in our veins, leaves have chlorophyll. It is when a leaf's "blood" is poured out that it changes colors.

Isn't that what Jesus did for us? He poured out His lifeblood for us to bring us joy, to put beauty back into our lives, to give us life itself!

THERE IS POWER IN THE BLOOD

Would you be whiter, much
whiter than snow?
There's pow'r in the blood,
pow'r in the blood;
Sinstains are lost in its
life-giving flow;
There's wonderful pow'r
in the blood.

There is pow'r, pow'r,
wonder-working pow'r
In the blood of the Lamb;
There is pow'r, pow'r,
wonder-working pow'r
In the precious blood
of the Lamb.

"Come now, and let us
reason together, saith the
Lord: though your sins be as
scarlet, they shall be as white
as snow" (Isaiah 1:18).

Throughout the Bible snow is used as a symbol for purity, the absence of any stains from sin. What Peter, James and John saw when Jesus was transformed on the Mount of Transfiguration was *"His raiment became shining, exceeding white as snow" (Mark 9:3).* The disciples that night were granted a sight of King Jesus in His heavenly robes.

Likewise, what the Marys saw when they arrived at the tomb, expecting to prepare Jesus for burial, was an angel described as having a *"countenance like lightning, and a raiment white as snow" (Matthew 28:3).*

What this hymnwriter says so powerfully is that our heavenly Father offers to clothe us in heavenly snow-robes as well. He pours the blood of Jesus over us in our sin-stained scarlet condition. We then rise up from that life-giving flow brightly white, brightly lit like the sunshine glistening on new fallen snow.

"Wash me, and I shall be whiter than snow"
(Psalm 51:7).

JUST A CLOSER WALK WITH THEE

I am weak but Thou art strong;
Jesus, keep me from all wrong;
I'll be satisfied as long
As I walk, let me walk close to Thee.

Just a closer walk with Thee,
Grant it, Jesus, is my plea,
Daily, walking close to Thee,
Let it be, dear Lord, let it be.

What lies around that curve in the road of life ahead of you? Of course you cannot possibly know if you have never travelled it before, if you have no map to show you. But what if a Friend were willing to accompany you? What if you had a Friend who not only knew the road, but who also had created you for the very purpose of travelling this course you now find yourself on?

Well, that is a part of the Gospel of Jesus Christ our Lord. He is the Friend who will join us on the way. He is the Friend who will shine His light on the path so that we know where to safely place our feet. He is the Friend who created us for His good purpose, and who is always waiting for our invitation to Him so that He can join us for a closer, closer walk.

"There is a friend that sticketh closer than a brother"
(Proverbs 18:24)

BLESSED ASSURANCE

Blessed assurance, Jesus is mine!
O what a foretaste of glory divine!
Heir of salvation, purchase of God,
Born of His Spirit, washed in His blood.

This is my story, this is my song,
Praising my Savior all the day long;
This is my story this is my song,
Praising my Savior all the day long.

"And if I go and prepare a place for you, I will come again, and receive you unto myself;
that where I am, there ye may be also" (John 14:3).

Daily we hike over the mountains and down into the valleys of our lives. Some days it seems as though we will always be on an uphill slope, with a thorn-infested, winding narrow path limiting our view of what could possibly lie ahead.

Then we suddenly round a corner in life and God gives us the refreshing vision of a gentle waterfall cascading into a cool pool of crystal clear water. "O what a foretaste of glory divine!" we cry out with the hymn writer. We see a slight glimpse of that heavenly place which Jesus continues to prepare for us.

"This is my story! This is my song!" Today, let's hear again the story, let's sing again the song. Let's tell of the blessed assurance we have. Let's assure others that Jesus always has been, is now and always will be right there for us all, whenever and wherever we need Him.

COUNT YOUR BLESSINGS

When you look at others with their lands of gold,
Think that Christ has promised you
His wealth untold;
Count your many blessings, money cannot buy
Your reward in heaven, nor your home on high.

Count your blessings, name them one by one;
Count your blessings, see what God hath done;
Count your blessings, name them one by one;
Count your blessings see what God hath done.

God does desire to bless us, to bless us richly.
He wants to, and in fact He already has *"blessed*
us with all spiritual blessings in heavenly places in
Christ" (Ephesians 1:3).

Our loving heavenly Father always
blesses us with exactly what we need. He blesses
us with a home, with the beauty of His creation,
with a church family where we can be blessed
and where we can be a blessing to others.
Let's make each day a day of
thanksgiving; a day when we count our
blessings and offer joyous praise
to the great Jehovah Jirah,
our provider God.

LOVE LIFTED ME

All my heart to Him I give,
Ever to Him I'll cling,
In His blessed presence live,
Ever His praises sing;
Love so mighty and so true
Merits my soul's best songs;
Faithful, loving service, too,
To Him belongs.

Love lifted me!
Love lifted me!
When nothing else could help,
Love lifted me!
Love lifted me!
Love lifted me!
When nothing else could help,
Love lifted me!

"I beseech you, therefore, brethren, by the mercies of God, that ye present your bodies a living sacrifice, holy, acceptable unto God, which is your reasonable service" (Romans 12:1).

As Paul says, and as the hymnist says, it is quite reasonable for us to give our hearts to God for what He has done for us. It is quite reasonable for us us to give Him our highest praises, our best songs, our minds, bodies and spirits for faithful, loving service.

It is reasonable because of what His love has done for us. Once mired in sin, we are now lifted above the cares of this world to dwell in the peaceful realm of His grace. His love has lifted us, and nothing can separate us from it!

Oh, Lord, I do thank You that Your love lifted me!

OLD TIME RELIGION

Give me that old time religion,
Give me that old time religion,
Give me that old time religion,
It's good enough for me.

The settlers in the Smokies faced tremendous difficulties as they sought to make a new life for themselves in America. The one constant in their lives was their old time religion, a religion firmly founded on their faith in a never-changing God.

No matter how difficult life became, they kept on because they knew God's word would always sustain them. They knew that what was good enough for Abraham, what was good enough for Moses, what was good enough for Paul and Silas was good enough for them. They had God's promises to stand on.

"The grass withereth, and the flower thereof falleth away, but the word of the Lord endureth forever" (I Peter 1:24, 25).

THERE SHALL BE SHOWERS OF BLESSING

"There shall be showers of blessing"
This is the promise of love;
There shall be seasons refreshing,
Sent from the Savior above.

"There shall be showers of blessing"
Precious reviving again;
Over the hills and the valleys,
Sound of abundance of rain.

Showers of blessing,
Showers of blessing we need;
Mercy drops round us are falling,
But for the showers we plead.

"And I will make them and the places round about my hill
a blessing; and I will cause the shower to come down in his season;
there shall be showers of blessing" (Ezekiel 34:26).

What a wonderful promise from God this is! He knows the seasons of our lives. He knows when we feel the cold winds of winter, and when we are drained by summer's blistering heat. Because He knows and cares so much for us, He promises to refresh us in each of those seasons by showering us with His blessings.

What a wonderful promise!
What a wonderful God we serve!

JESUS LOVES ME

Jesus loves me! this I know,
For the Bible tells me so;
Little ones to Him belong,
They are weak but He is
strong.

Jesus loves me! He who died
Heaven's gates to open wide;
He will wash away my sin,
Let His little child come in.

Yes, Jesus loves me!
Yes, Jesus loves me!
Yes, Jesus loves me!
The Bible tells me so.

It is the most simple of messages; simple so that little children can understand and respond. "Jesus loves me," the song and Holy Scripture say. He loves me and you so much that *"while we were yet sinners, Christ died for us" (Romans 5:8)*. Yes, Jesus loves us, and all we need is a child-like faith to receive the many benefits which that love bestows.

When we are weak, His love will strengthen us to go on believing. When we are weak, His Holy Spirit will always be with us to remind us of what the Bible says: "Jesus loves me. Yes! Jesus loves me!"